DOUGLAS A-4C/L IN U.S. MARINE SERVICE

Above, the first Navy or Marine squadron to equip with the A4D-2N was VMA-225 which received its first aircraft, BuNo 145086, on 11 March 1960. Shown here is BuNo 145104 CE/13 loaded out with 18 Mk. 82 bombs. This aircraft was acquired on 5 April 1960. (John Elliott collection)

THE A4D-2N/A-4C: In September 1957, the Navy allowed Douglas to pursue a limited all-weather fix for the Skyhawk. This became the A4D-2N or A-4C in 1962. The AN/APG-53A from the A4D-3 proposal was installed as was an AN/AJB-3 all-attitude flight reference and bombing system, an automatic flight control system, and an improved AN/ASN-19A navigation computer.

The avionics changes required a major re-alignment of the cockpit. The principal problem was to find room for the 5-inch square AJB-3 display. The armament panel was moved downward and the instruments and controls were rearranged on the instrument panel.

The aircraft's structure changed about 15%, which included the nose and refueling probe to be stretched 9-inches. Although the J52 was planned, the A-4C ended up with a J65-W-20 engine of 8,300lbs thrust and an overall empty weight of 9,728lbs.

Initially, besides the lengthened nose, the A4D-2N could easily be discerned by its black radome. This design was changed to a paintable dielectric material with a white or black erosion-resistant area on the tip of the nose. These were retrofitted to all A4D-2Ns as were windshield wipers on or about the same time. Also during production, the 5 liter liquid oxygen system was replaced with a 10 liter unit and the engine oil capacity also was increased.

The A4D-2N was equipped with a Douglas Escapac I ejection seat that provided for a ground level ejection at speeds above 90 knots. Its sides were extended upwards and forwards, the seat support system and inertia reel were improved, and a safety lever was added to the front of the headrest. The units also were retrofitted to all A4D-1 and A4D-2 Skyhawks.

Although I would classify the A4D-2N/A-4C an interim design in the Skyhawk series, it was the most prolific with 638 airframes produced. These were BuNos 145062-145146, 147669-147849, 148304-148317, 148435-148612, 149487-149646, 150581-150600.

THE A-4L: The A-4L was an upgraded A-4C with electronic and hardware changes that would emulate the A-4F. The A-4L had the fuselage hump found on most A-4Fs added to the A-4Cs to house the new avionics. Another addition was the installation of lift spoilers to the wings. Douglas modified one A-4C, BuNo 148307, into the first A-4L. Its first flight was conducted on 21 August 1969. The reserves then received 99 conversion kits which were installed at the Naval Air Rework Facilities (NARFs). The 100 A-4Ls were BuNos 145065, 145076-145078, 145092, 145101, 145103, 145114, 145117, 145119, 145121-145122, 145128, 145133, 145141, 147669, 147671, 147690, 147703, 147706, 147708, 147717, 147723, 147727, 147736, 147750, 147754, 147761, 147768, 147772, 147780, 147782, 147787, 147793, 147796, 147798, 147802, 147807, 147815, 147825, 147827, 147836, 147843, 148306, 148307, 148316, 148436, 148446, 148453, 148479, 148487, 148490, 148498, 148505, 148530, 148538, 148555, 148578, 148581, 148586, 148588, 148600, 148602, 148611, 149497, 149500, 149502, 149506, 149508, 149516, 149518, 149531, 149532, 149536, 149539, 149540, 149551, 149555, 149556, 149569, 149573, 149579, 149583, 149591, 149593, 149595, 149604, 149607, 149608, 149620, 149623, 149626, 149630, 149633, 149635, 149640, 149646, 150586, 150593, and 150598.

HEADQUARTERS & MAINTENANCE SQUADRON FIFTEEN, H&MS-15

The unit was established on 1 March 1942 at Camp Kearney, San Diego, CA, as Headquarters and Service Squadron 15. On 1 July 1942, the squadron was redesignated Headquarters Squadron 15 and on 24 February 1954 the squadron became Headquarters and Maintenance Squadron 15 (H&MS-15). In August 1966, the squadron was transferred from MCAS El Toro to MCAF Iwakuni, Japan, from where the squadron supported the Vietnam War.

MCAS El Toro-based H&MS-15 received one A4D-2N (A-4C), BuNo 147783, on 30 September 1960. It was in custody for only one month. Nineteen more were acquired in 1961 and all were transferred out within two months of their recipt. Twenty-one more were acquired and disposed of in a similar fashion in 1962, 1963, and 1964, but four A-4Cs were deployed as a fighter cover Det for an ASW carrier in 1965 and 1966.

H&MS-15 deployed Det N aboard the USS Hornet (CVS-12) from 12 August 1965 through 23 March 1966 as part of CVSG-57. During the cruise, CVS-12 spent 80 days on the line off Vietnam. The four A-4Cs used during the deployment were named after hookers: BuNo 147681 YV/81 was "Fanny Hill", 147809 YV/82 was "Polly Adler", 147829 YV/83 was "Mame Stover", and 148464 YV/84 was "Ko Sisters". These four aircraft also flew operations from the carriers Ticonderoga, Midway and Ranger during the cruise.

Below, the six H&MS-15 Det N pilots (left-to-right; Capt Tommy W. Green, 1st LT Steve L. Brown, 1st LT Walley F. Leo, Capt Hank C. Ivy, Capt D.E.T Wilson and Capt Roger T. Lininger pose in front of A-4C, BuNo 147681 YV/81 "Fanny Hill", aboard (CVS-12) in 1965. Note the 27 mission marks and the VA-22 logo aft of the intake with VMA-22 beneath it. (USN via Tailhook)

Above, H&MS-15 Det N A-4C, BuNo 148464 YV/84 "Ko Sisters" prior to launch. (USN) Above right, Sidewinder armed BuNo 147829 YV/83 "Mame Stover". (USN) Below, 148464 takes the barrier and loses its nose aboard CVA-41. (USN)

MARINE ATTACK TRAINING SQUADRON, VMAT-102 "SKYHAWKS"

VMAT-102 was activated with A-4Cs on 1 January 1969 and started the attack training syllabus in May. The syllabus emphasis was:

A.) Weapons delivery with instruction on ground targets.
B.) Technical training for maintenance personnel.
C.) Close air support.
D.) Armed reconnaissance.
E.) Helicopter support.
F.) S.A.T.S. training.
G.) Conduct O.R.I.

An A-4L, BuNo 147669, was received on 10 March 1970 and operated through 18 May 1970. All but three A-4Cs were replaced with A-4Es and later TA-4Js by the summer of 1970. The last three were transferred out successively on 26 September 1970, 10 November 1970, and 28 January 1971. A-4Fs were added in August 1973 and the A-4M in 1975. The unit was deactivated in 1987.

The squadron lost three A-4Cs, BuNo 148474, 148508, and 148472. LT Graham E. Tharp was killed while flying 148474 on 23 April 1969 while attempting a crash landing after being unable to eject from the plane. When the Skyhawk hit the ground the seat ejected and Tharp was killed. 148472 was stricken at Yuma due to fatigue on 10 November 1970 and 147731 was stricken at NAS Jacksonville after inspection before overhaul.

From May 1969 through September 1973, the squadron established a safety record of 40,000 accident free hours in the Skyhawk. They were the only tactical jet squadron to reach that figure up to that point in time.

Above, VMAT-102 A-4C, BuNo 145119 SC/1, at NAS Alameda, CA, in April 1969. (Mark Aldrich collection) Below, VMAT-102 A-4C, BuNo 148494 SC/4, at NAS Alameda, CA, in July 1969. Fuselage and tail trim were red. (Mark Aldrich collection) Bottom, VMAT-102 A-4C, BuNo 145103 SC/17, at Alameda in July 1969. (Mark Aldrich collection)

MARINE ATTACK SQUADRON ONE-TWO-ONE, VMA-121 "GREEN KNIGHTS"

Marine Fighting Squadron 121 (VMF-121) was activated on 24 June 1941 at MCAS Quantico, VA, and equipped with the Grumman F4F Wildcat. During WWII, the unit operated from Guadalcanal and produced such aces as Joe Foss. They returned to the United States briefly, before redeploying into combat with the Vought/Goodyear F4U/FG Corsair. By the end of WWII, VMF-121 was credited with 208 air-to-air kills, the highest score of any Marine unit. The squadron was deactivated on 9 September 1945 and remained dormant until 1 July 1946, when they were reactivated at NAS Glenview, IL, and equipped with the F8F-1 Bearcat and the F4U-4 Corsair.

With the outbreak of the Korean War, the unit returned to active duty as a Marine Attack Squadron on 15 May 1951, and was equipped with the AD-2 Skyraider. Known as the "Wolf Raiders" and "Heavy Haulers", the unit supported Allied operations in North and South Korea. They remained at Pyong-Taek (K-6) until 1957, when they moved to MCAS El Toro, CA, and re-equipped with F9F-8B Cougars.

The Green Knights transitioned to the Douglas A4D-2 Skyhawk in 1959. The following year, they deployed aboard the USS Coral Sea (CVA-43) for a WestPac cruise, returning in the spring of 1961.

They transitioned to the A4D-2N (A-4C) in April 1961. Three aircraft (BuNos 148464, 148465 and 148474) were received on 12 April, and three more (148486, 148493 and 148494) were acquired on the 14th. Another nine (148451, 148453, 148462, 148467, 148469, 148471, 148472, 148475, and 148477) arrived on 17 April, bringing the squadron strength up to fifteen A4D-2Ns.

During training on their new A4D-2Ns, the squadron conducted Field Mirror Landing Practice on the SATS field at MCB Twenty-Nine Palms, CA. On 19 July 1962, 1st LT James Sauer in BuNo 148560 ran off the runway at El Toro and into the perimeter fence because of a stuck throttle. He was uninjured and walked away from his plane. BuNo 148561 crashed after an engine fire on 1 November 1962 eight miles Northwest of MCAS Yuma, AZ. The pilot, MAJ William W. Bryant, was chasing LT Garrett McClanahan on a FAM flight when he ejected safely. In November 1962, after this incident, VMA-121 deployed its A-4Cs to NAS Cecil Field, FL, to relieve CVG-10 during the Cuban Missile Crisis. The assignment only lasted for a one month period, while the squadron was on 24-hour constant combat alert. On 27 November, Capt John MacDonald Moore was killed when BuNo 147713 crashed and burned near Palatka, FL, while stationed at Cecil Field.

LtCOL W.E. Sparling relieved LCOL L.M. Mckleson on 19 April 1963 and the squadron conducted extensive training at MCAS Yuma, AZ, in preparation for the squadron's deployment to Japan. On 7 December 1963, while flying from Yuma, MAJ Thomas S. Oden was killed when he crashed 35 miles south of Gila Bend, AZ, while on the gunnery range.

VMA-121 deployed their A-4Cs to Japan in March 1964. They operated out of Itazuke AB, Naha, Kadena, and Iwakuni and deployed to Cubi Point, Okinawa, Osan AB, and Hong Kong. Bomb and rocket training was conducted at Ashiya and low level and loft bombing training were accomplished at Tori-Jima and Koon-Ni.

The A-4E, replaced the A-4Cs on the squadrons return to El Toro, CA, on 5 April 1965 and the squadron transferred to MCAS Cherry Point on 1 February 1969. While flying the A-

Below, all 15 A4D-2Ns initially assigned to VMA-121 at El Toro in April 1961. Radomes and fin tips were black. (Harry Gann)

4C, VMA-121 conducted carrier qualifications aboard the USS Yorktown, USS Ticonderoga, USS Kitty Hawk, and the USS Coral Sea.

Above, VMA-121 A4D-2N, BuNo 148493 VK/6, makes a JATO take-off from El Toro in 1961 with 12 bombs and a centerline drop tank. Fin tip and radome were black. (USMC via Mark Aldrich) Below, VMA-121 A-4C, BuNo 147752 VK/12, at Iwakuni, Japan, in 1964. (via E.S. Holmburg) Bottom, same aircraft with squadronmate VK/11 in the background. (via E.S. Holmburg)

MARINE ATTACK SQUADRON ONE - TWO - THREE, VMA-123

Marine Fighter Squadron One Twenty-Three (VMF-123) was established on 7 September 1942 with F4U-1Ds. The squadron was disestablished after the war on 10 September 1945. VMF-123 was reactivated on 15 April 1958 at NAS Los Alamitos, CA, as a reserve fighter squadron flying the F9F Cougar along with VMF-134. On 1 July 1962, VMF-123 was redesignated Marine Attack Squadron One Twenty-Three (VMA-123) while equipped with F9F-8Bs. They then began flying A-4A/Bs until being replaced by A-4Cs starting in December 1969. The A-4Cs (tail code 5L) were only in service for a little over six months. Of the twenty-eight A-4Cs assigned, all but three were re-assigned to VA-303 (5), VA-304 (4), and VA-305 (16) with the reorganization of the reserves in July 1970. Of the other three, one went to MARTD Jacksonville on 28 February 1970, one was converted to a A-4L in April 1970 and one was held at Los Alamitos until January 1971 when it went to MASDC.

MARINE ATTACK SQUADRON ONE-TWO-FOUR, VMA-124 "WHISTLING DEATH"

The squadron was formed on 7 September 1942 at Camp Kearny, CA, with remnants of VMF-121. They became the first Marine squadron to utilize the Vought F4U-1 Corsair. The Death's Head squadron (later the Checkerboards) arrived on Guadalcanal on 11 February 1943 and participated in the Russell Island, New Georgia, and Vella Lavella campaigns. The squadron returned to the West Coast in October of 1943 where they remained until September 1944, when they moved to Pearl Harbor, TH. They boarded the USS Essex (CV-9) on 28 December 1944 and supported the Lingayen landings, Iwo Jima landings,

Above, VMA-124 A-4L, BuNo 145117 5M/108, at Richards-Gebaur AFB on 10 April 1971. (Fred Roos) Below, VMA-124 A-4L, BuNo 149540 5M/107, at Richards-Gebaur AFB on 10 April 1971. (Fred Roos)

and attacked Tokyo and Okinawa. The squadron returned to the West Coast in April 1945, before redeploying to Ewa, TH, in September. Following the surrender of the Japanese, the squadron returned to El Toro, CA, where it was deactivated on 31 January 1946.

The squadron was reactivated as the "Whistling Death" Squadron at NAS Memphis, TN, and assigned the F4U-4 Corsair, from which it derived its name. VMF-124 became the first squadron to reach full strength under the Marine Air Reserve Training Command. As VMF-124, the squadron transitioned to F9F-6 Cougars and then FJ-4B Furies.

The unit was redesignated VMA-124 on 1 May 1965 and equipped with the A-4A/B Skyhawk. These were replaced with A-4Ls in early 1970 and were supplemented with A-4Es in 1979. In 1985, the A-4M replaced the squadron's A-4Es. In 1994, the unit, less aircraft, moved to NAS Fort Worth Joint Reserve Base (JRB), TX, where it became a paper squadron. It was redesignated VMFA-124 and assigned to MAG-41 before being deactivated in 1997 without ever receiving aircraft.

Above, VMA-124 A-4L, BuNo 149540 QP/107, at NAS Memphis, TN, on 14 October 1973. Rudder trim was red with dark blue segments. Fuselage stripes were red-white-blue. (Fred Roos) At left, VMA-124 A-4L, BuNo 149646 QP/106, touches down at NAS Willow Grove in June 1974. The diagonal red-white-blue fuselage stripe has all but faded away. (Norm Taylor collection) Bottom, VMA-124 A-4L, BuNo 149532 QP/112, taxis at NAS Willow Grove, IL, in June 1974. (Norm Taylor collection)

MARINE ATTACK SQUADRON ONE-THREE-ONE, VMA-131 "DIAMONDBACKS"

One of the oldest units in Marine Aviation, the squadron began life as VMS-1 and became VMSB-131 in July 1941. Flying the SB2U-3 Vindicator, the unit moved to MCAS Ewa in September 1942, and became the first Marine torpedo bombing squadron when they transitioned to the Grumman TBF-1 Avenger. The unit moved to Guadalcanal and Espiritu Santo in November 1942. The squadron was redesignated VMTB-131 in June 1943 and returned to the US. After retraining new personnel, they returned to the South Pacific in April 1944 and supported operations against Okinawa in May after which the squadron was deactivated on 16 November 1945.

The squadron was reactivated on 15 April 1958 in the Marine Corps reserves and located at Floyd Bennett Field, NY, as VMF-131. Initially flying the F9F-6 Cougar and the FJ-3 Fury, they traded-up to FJ-4Bs before acquiring A-4A/Bs in 1965 and becoming VMA-131 before receiving A-4Cs in October 1969 (5R tail code). In September 1970, Floyd Bennett Field closed and VMA-131

Above, VMA-131 A-4C, BuNo 145083 5R/10, on 11 June 1970 with faded Floyd Bennett Field 5R tail code and ex-VA-72 markings bleeding through. (Roger Besecker) Below, VMA-131 A-4C, BuNo 148605 5W/2, at NAS Willow Grove on 11 June 1970. Rudder was red with orange-yellow segments and drop tank tips were red with a orange-yellow stripe. (Roger Besecker) Bottom, VMA-131 A-4C, BuNo 147841 5W/06, landing at Willow Grove, PA, in January 1971. (Norm Taylor collection)

transferred to NAS Willow Grove, PA (5W tail code then QG). In the summer of 1973, VMA-131 along with VMA-133 and VMA-142 CarQualed for three days aboard the USS Independence.

The squadron lost four A-4Cs during its tenure. They were BuNos 147822, 150596, 147735, and 149989. 147822, piloted by Capt. Charles B. Coltrin, crashed on a farm in NC on 23 July 1973 and ejected safely. 150596 was making a GCA approach to Willow Grove when heavy vibrations forced Capt. R.W. Strasburg to eject safely on 8 May 1973. 147735 crashed into a wooded hillside after MAJ Ralph S. Dilullo ejected safely from his failing jet on 1 March 1975. Finally, 149989 exploded at about 500 feet altitude shortly after take-off, killing Capt. Robert M. Baker.

In March 1975, the A-4E began replacing the A-4Cs and A-4Fs were added in 1980 with the A-4M replacing both versions in 1988. The Diamondbacks relinquished their A-4Ms in 1994 and became a paper squadron until their deactivation in 1997.

Above, VMA-131 A-4C, BuNo 148569 QG/05, at NAS Miramar, CA, in May 1971. (USMC) Below, VMA-131 A-4C, BuNo 147779 QG/12, landing in May 1972. Bottom, VMA-131 A-4C, BuNo 149587 QG/00, landing in February 1975. (all Norm Taylor collection)

MARINE ATTACK SQUADRON ONE-THREE-THREE, VMA-133 "DRAGONS"

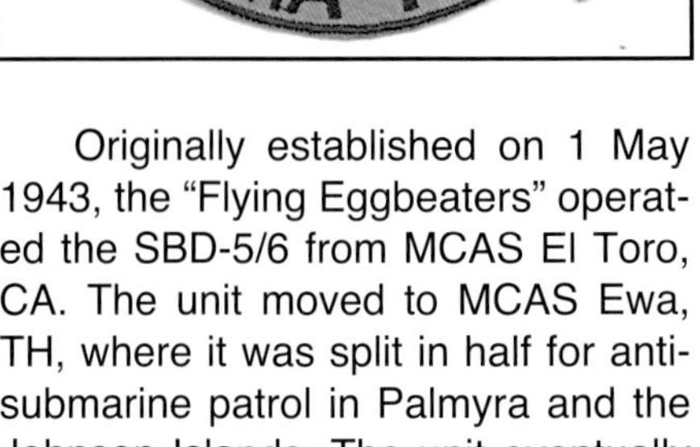

Originally established on 1 May 1943, the "Flying Eggbeaters" operated the SBD-5/6 from MCAS El Toro, CA. The unit moved to MCAS Ewa, TH, where it was split in half for anti-submarine patrol in Palmyra and the Johnson Islands. The unit eventually moved to Torokina in the summer of 1944, and carried out missions against the Japanese at Bouganville and New Britain until December, when the unit was moved to Emirau. The squadron supported operations into the Philippines until the end of the war. They were deactivated on 1 August 1945.

Above, variation of squadron patch used on VMA-133 A-4Cs. (Fred Roos) Below, VMA-133 A-4C, BuNo 147722 5G/4, at NAS Alameda, CA, on 18 July 1970. Rudder was red with orange-yellow segments. (Fred Roos) Bottom, VMA-133 A-4C, BuNo 148480 5G/00, assigned to the MAG-49 CO on 9 October 1971. (Fred Roos)

The unit was reactivated as VMF-133 in the 1950s as a reserve squadron at NAS Oakland, CA. Their first jet aircraft was the McDonnell F2H-2 Banshee followed in 1959 by the F2H-3/4 Big Banjo. In 1961, the squadron transitioned to the Douglas A4D-1 Skyhawk and the squadron moved to NAS Alameda, CA. The A4D-2/A-4B began arriving in 1962 and the A-4C in early 1970. Initially, the A-4Cs wore "5G" tail codes before receiving "ME" tail codes in 1971-72. The A-4Cs were replaced with A-4Fs in 1976 and in turn were replaced with A-4Ms in 1989. VMA-133 was deactivated in 1992.

Above, VMA-133 A-4C, BuNo 148528 ME/5, at NAS Alameda, CA, on 18 October 1975. (Fred Roos) Below, VMA-133 A-4C, BuNo 147675 ME/00, at NAS Alameda, CA, in October 1975. (Swisher) Bottom, VMA-133 A-4C, BuNo 148610 ME/13, in bicenntenial markings at NAS Alameda, CA, in March 1977. Rudder was red-white-blue. Insignia aft of the intake says "Bay Area Golden Gaters". (Swisher)

MARINE ATTACK SQUADRON ONE - THREE - FOUR, VMA-134 "HAWKS"

VMSB-134 was established on 1 May 1943 at MCAS Santa Barbara, CA, and flew the Douglas SBD-3. The following month, they were redesignated VMTB-134 when they upgraded to the TBF/TBM Avenger. They deployed to Espiritu Santo in October and began pounding the Japanese on Bougainville. VMTB-134 became the first squadron to use airborne forward firing rockets in combat during operations against Rabaul on 17 February 1944. For that distiction, they named the unit the "Rockettes". During the spring of 1944, they flew strikes against Rabaul and Kaveing and provided anti-submarine patrols out of Peleliu until the end of the war. After the war, the unit joined MAG-32 in Tsingtao, China, in October 1945. VMTB-134 was deactivated on 30 April 1946.

VMF-134 was reactivated as a reserve squadron at NAS Los Alamitos, CA, on 15 April 1958, and was equipped with Grumman F9F-6/7/8 Cougars. They were redesignated VMA-134 on 1 July 1962 and equipped with the A-4A Skyhawk. By 1965, they were flying both A-4As and A-4Bs. They upgraded to the A-4C in late 1969 ("5L" tail code) and transferred to MCAS El Toro, CA, in 1971 when Los Alamitos was deactivated and made a Joint Reserve Base (JRB). In 1971, the "5L" tail code was briefly changed to "QV" before progressing to "MF" in 1972. The A-4F replaced the A-4C in 1976 and the F-4N replaced the A-4Fs on 1 October 1983. The F/A-18 Hornet replaced the Phantoms in July 1969.

Below, VMA-134 A-4C, BuNo 150588 5L/3, at NAS Los Alamitos, CA, on 15 July 1970. (Fred Roos) Bottom, VMA-134 A-4C, BuNo 148575 5L/18, at Los Alamitos in 1970. Rudder was green. (Ginter collection)

VMA-134 "HAWKS"

Above, VMA-134 A-4C, BuNo 145135 5L/12, at NAS Los Alamitos, CA, on 15 July 1970. Rudder was green. (Fred Roos) At left, VMA-134 A-4C, BuNo 149541 QV/9, in 1972. Rudder was red with white segments. (Harry Gann) Bottom, VMA-134 A-4C, BuNo 149605 MF/3, at MCAS El Toro in May 1974. Rudder was red with white segments. The Hawk on the fuselage side was black. (Harry Gann)

MARINE ATTACK SQUADRON ONE-FOUR-TWO, VMA-142 "FLYING GATORS"

VMSB-142 was activated on 1 March 1942 at Camp Kearny, CA. After deploying to Guadalcanal in October 1942, the unit flew anti-submarine patrols in the Espiritu Santo area. The squadron moved to the Fiji Islands on 23 April 1943 before moving to Emirau in September. They supported operations in the Philippines until 21 September 1945, when they were deactivated at MCAS Ewa, TH.

VMF-142 was reactivated on 1 July 1946 as part of the Marine Reserves at MCAS Miami, FL. While flying the F9F-8B Cougar, the squadron was redesignated VMA-142 on 15 May 1958. The squadron moved to NAS Jacksonville, FL, in 1959 and transitioned to the A-4B Skyhawk in 1964.

In late 1969 ("5F" tail code), A-4Cs were acquired and flown for a year until being replaced with A-4Ls

Below, VMA-142 A-4L, BuNo 149626 5F/1, at Randolph AFB, TX, on 28 August 1971. Rudder was trimmed in red and orange-yellow. Tips of drop tanks were red. (Bob Mills via Norm Taylor) Bottom, VMA-142 A-4L, BuNo 148446 MB/12, receiving maintenance in March 1973. Rudder was red with orange-yellow segments. (Ken Buchanan)

Above, VMA-142 A-4L, BuNo 149626 MB/00, on 10 October 1973. (Fred Roos) At left, VMA-142 A-4L, BuNo 147815 MB/7, at NAS Jacksonville, FL, on 10 December 1975. (L.B. Sides via Mark Aldrich) Below left, VMA-142 A-4L, BuNo 147807 MB/9, in 1975 with blue rudder and white stars. (Lionel Paul) Bottom, VMA-142 A-4L, BuNo 147815 MB/7, at Dobbins AFB, GA, on 23 October 1975 in red-white-blue bicentennial markings. (Bill Sides via Paul Minert)

in late 1970. VMA-142 went aboard the USS Independence in August of 1971, along with pilots from VMA-131 and VMA-133 for three days of carrier qualifications. In late 1971, the squadron's tail code was changed from "5F" to "MB" and in 1976 A-4Fs replaced the A-4Ls. In late 1978, they transitioned to A-4Ms and moved to NAS Cecil Field, FL. As VMFA-142 they transitioned to the F/A-18A Hornet on 21 December 1990.

MARINE ATTACK SQUADRON TWO - ONE - ONE, VMA-211 "WAKE ISLAND AVENGERS"

The unit began as VF-4M on 1 January 1937 at NAS San Diego, CA, equipped with a half-dozen Grumman F3F-1 biplane fighters and a mixture of SU-4s, O3U-1s, SBC-3s and F2F-1s. They were redesignated VMF-2 on 1 January 1937. VMF-2 became the first Marine unit to deploy aboard a carrier, en mass, when they took their F3F-2s aboard the USS Ranger (CV-4) in 1938.

The unit moved to MCAS Ewa, TH, in January 1941. They were redesignated VMF-211 in July, and transitioned to the F4F Wildcat in September. With the deterioration of US/Japanese relations, a detachment of VMF-211 was moved to Wake Island on 4 December 1941. Three days later, the island was attacked by Japanese Naval Forces. After fierce fighting, the aircraft were decimated, and all remaining aviation personnel engaged the enemy in hand-to-hand combat. The remaining forces surren-

Above, VMA-211 A4D-2N, BuNo 145119 CF/16, on display with a full bomb load. (Ginter collection) Below, VMA-211 A4D-1, BuNo 142189 CF/1, at left poses with its replacement the A4D-2N, BuNo 145065 CF/4, at MCAS El Toro, CA, in April 1960 with a VMA-311 A-4B, BuNo 142882 WL/19, in the middle. (Harry Gann) Bottom, VMA-211 A4D-2N, BuNo 145065 CF/4, in April 1960. (Clay Jansson)

Above, VMA-211 A-4C, BuNo 148469 CF/10, launches from the USS Oriskany (CVA-34) in January 1962. (Paul Dros via Tailhook) Below, VMA-211 A-4C, BuNo 145101 CF/19, landing in Japan in 1962-63. Rudder segments and nose stripe were red. (Ginter collection) Bottom, VMA-211 A-4Cs in flight in 1961. (Mark Aldrich collection)

dered on 23 December 1941.

VMF-211 was quickly reorganized at Ewa, and adopted the name, “Wake Island Avengers”. Equipped with the F4F-4, the unit was moved to Palmyra Island for anti-submarine patrols. They returned to Hawaii in June 1943 and transitioned to the Vought F4U-1 Corsair. After training for several weeks, the unit was moved to the South Pacific, where they engaged the enemy at Guadalcanal and Bougainville. The unit was moved to Leyte in December 1944 to support operations in the Philippines. The Avengers ended the war with 91 enemy planes shot down, and supported the occupation process from Peiping, China, in 1945. After deploying aboard the USS Rendova (CVE-114) from November 1948 to May 1949, the unit moved to MCAS Edenton (later Cherry Point).

The squadron was redesignated VMA-211 on 1 July 1952 and traded in their Corsairs for AD-2 Skyraiders. By 1954, they were flying AD-4/4Bs which were replaced with A4D-2 Skyhawks beginning on 9 September 1957. In late 1958, squadron personnel transferred to Iwakuni, Japan, where they relieved VMA-224 and acquired their A4D-1 aircraft. VMA-224 returned to Cherry Point, NC, and took control of the former VMA-211 A4D-2 aircraft. On VMA-211's return to CONUS in 1959, they were transferred to MCAS El Toro, CA, where they transitioned to the A4D-2N in March 1960.

VMA-211 lost three A4D-2N aircraft. Two, BuNos 147791 and 148477, were involved in a mid-air shortly after the two simultaneously took off from El Toro on 8 August 1961. Capt. Hugh W. Bergey and 2nd LT Nolvie M. Adams were both killed when their planes crashed into the ridge about 1.5 miles from base. The third A-4C was lost near the Nevada-Arizona state line on 18 December 1961 when 1st LT R.C. Bradfield ejected safely.

In March 1962, VMA-211 conducted the first Skyhawk squadron trans-pac from El Toro, CA, to Iwakuni, Japan. The route included Kaneohe, Wake, Midway, and Guam. While stationed in Japan, VMA-211 made several deployments to Okinawa and the Philippines. Also, in May 1962, about 24 support personnel were sent TAD to Ubon, Thailand to assist VMA-332 in maintaining their aircraft during close air support sorties into Laos. In March 1963, the squadron returned to El Toro.

In 1964, they transitioned to the A-4E and in September 1976 they re-equipped with the A-4M. The squadron moved to Yuma in 1997 where they replaced their Skyhawks with AV-8Bs by 21 February 1990.

MARINE ATTACK SQUADRON TWO-ONE-FOUR, VMA-214 "BLACKSHEEP"

Above, VMA-214 A-4C, BuNo 147788 WE/8, on a mission over Vietnam. (USMC) Below, VMA-214 CO, MAJ O'Keefe accepts the Martin "Top Shot" award on 2 September 1964 for the most accurate and reliable USN or USMC squadron with the Bullpup missile. (Dave Ekstrand) Bottom, "Pappy" Boyington visited VMA-214 at Chu Lai on 28 August 1965. Front row L-to-R, 1st LTs Lee Burns, Bill Fitts, Geo Focht, "Pappy", WO Will Williaford, Capt Bill Loftus and Capt Clancy Crigler. 2nd row, 1st LT Bill Bartlett and Capt Slats Combs. 3rd row, Capt Gomer Rooke, Capt Dave Sites, 1st LT Pete Wyrick, LCOL O'Keefe (CO), MAJ Bob Chapin, Capt Ed Baker, WO Darryl Smith, and Capt Gary Larson. (Dave Ekstrand)

VMF-214 was activated on 1 July 1942 at MCAS Ewa, TH, and equipped with Grumman F4F-4 Wildcats. The unit moved to Guadalcanal in March 1943 and transitioned to the Vought F4U-1 Corsair in June. With the new aircraft, the unit became known as the "Swashbucklers". After a combat tour in the Russell Islands, the squadron members went to Australia for a little R&R. Meanwhile, a Major attached to the Air Group borrowed 214's squadron number, obtained aircraft and pilots from the group's personnel pool and formed the most infamous Marine Squadron ever, "The BlackSheep". With MAJ Greg Boyington at the helm, the BlackSheep made numerous successful fighter sweeps over Rabaul. Shortly before the unit rotated back to the US, Boyington was shot down and taken prisoner.

VMF-214 arrived at MCAS Santa Barbara, CA, in January 1944 for rest and retraining. They returned to the Pacific theater aboard the USS Franklin (CV-13). The Franklin was bombed and nearly sunk, and the squadron regrouped at MCAAS El Centro, CA, where it was deactivated. During the war VMF-214 accounted for 127 enemy aircraft shot down.

VMF-214 was reactivated in 1948 and equipped with F4U-4s. The unit moved to Japan in July 1950 and boarded the USS Sicily with F4U-4Bs for operations against North Korea. VMF-214 moved to MCAS Kaneohe Bay, TH, and transitioned to the McDonnell F2H-4 Banshee. They were redesignated VMF(AW)-214 in December 1956 and deployed

VMA-214 "BLACKSHEEP"

Above, VMA-214 A-4C, BuNo 148559 WE/16, leaves Chu Li armed with Zuni rockets in 1965. (Ginter collection) At left, VMA-214 A-4C piloted by 1st LT Rex Thames was hit by a 57mm AA gun while bombing the Chepone Bridge on Highway Nine on 8 February 1966. The shell took off the upper fuselage down to the wing between the cockpit and the dorsal fin. Despite the damage, the aircraft made a safe recovery at Da Nang. (Dave Ekstrand) Bottom, pictured are Capt Lee Burns (L), LCOL Keith O'Keefe (CO), Capt Bob Melville (R), and Capt Ed Baker (standing) as they prepare for the squadron's last combat flight of their first rotation at Chu Li on 11 February 1966. By this time, the four pilots had amassed over 600 combat missions between them. (Dave Ekstrand)

aboard the USS Hancock (CVA-19) from April to September 1957. The unit transitioned to the North American FJ-4B Fury upon their return, and were redesignated VMA-214.

Under the command of LCOL R. Wullane, the BlackSheep transitioned to the Douglas A4D-2 Skyhawk in January 1962. The unit sent a detachment aboard the USS Hornet (CVS-12) from October 1963 to April 1964.

After returning to El Toro, the squadron traded in its A-4Bs for A-4Cs in March 1964 and on the 21st received the quarterly FMFPac safety award. This was followed by two weeks of intensive weapons training at MCAAS Yuma, AZ. On 2 September 1964, the squadron was presented the "Top Shot" award by the Martin Co. for their accuracy with the Bullpup air-to-ground missile. Squadron pilots beat out both Navy and Marine pilots from both coasts during routine training missions conducted during fiscal year 1964 to receive the award.

In early 1965, the squadron made two brief deployments to Kaneohe before boarding the USS Valley Forge (LPH-8) and the USS Snohomish County (LST-1126) for their transfer to MCAS Iwakuni, Japan, on 15 March 1965. At Iwakuni, VMA-214 traded their Skyhawks for those of VMA-121. On 23 April, the squadron deployed for weapons training to NAS Cubi Point, Philippines. The unit flew 700 hours of training in May and was ordered to Vietnam in June 1965.

VMA-214's CO, LCOL O'Keefe, lead the first BlackSheep division into the 4,000 feet of SATS runway at Chu Lai, Vietnam, on 21 June 1965. The squadron remained in Vietnam for eight months and flew 3,971 combat missions in 5,274 combat hours. In February 1966, the squadron rotated out of Vietnam and exchanged pilots and personnel before returning to Chu Lai on 1 May 1966 under the command of LCOL "Del" Davis. The unit was pulled out of Vietnam in May 1967, after flying over 13,000 sorties.

Above left, on 14 May 1966, Capt Ed Baker flew his 205th combat mission to become the first BlackSheep to pass the 200 mission mark in Vietnam. Baker spent ten months in country participating in Operations Starlight, Piranha, Harvest Moon, Mallard, Blue Marlin, and Double Eagle. His 205 missions totalled 275 hours of combat flying and earned him eleven Air Medals with a twelfth pending. (Dave Ekstrand)

Above right, VMA-214 A-4C leaves Chu Lai for another mission. (USMC) Below, stacked up bombs in front of a VMA-214 A-4C at Chu Lai. (Dave Ekstrand) Bottom, VMA-214 A-4C, BuNo 148597 WE/19, landing at NAS Atsugi, Japan, on 27 May 1966. Rudder was black with white stars. (Toyokazu Matsuzaki)

The following five incidents occurred while involved in the Vietnam War. On 24 September 1965, BuNo 148508 was heavily damaged when its pilot pulled out of a bombing run a little late and hit the the tree tops. 1st LT Rex Thames nursed his severely damaged A-4C back to Da Nang on 8 February 1966 after being hit by a 57mm AA gun while bombing the Chepone Bridge on Highway 9. On 28 March 1966,

Capt Jack D. Rothwell was killed during a night ordnance delivery training exercise in BuNo 145109. Then on, 12 May 1966, BuNo 148535, was damaged beyond repair when the pilot landed short at Chu Lai and left the runway. On 17 March 1967, another pilot,

Above, VMA-214 A-4C, BuNo 148531 WE/4, at NAS Alameda, CA, in July 1967 after the unit returned from Vietnam. The fuselage stripe was red. (William Swisher) Below, VMA-214 A-4C, BuNo 148436 WE/12, at MCAS El Toro, CA, in July 1969 at NAS Willow Grove, PA. (Roger Besecker) Bottom, VMA-214 A-4C, BuNo 145126 WE/7, at Van Nuys, CA, in July 1968. (Nick Williams)

Above, VMA-214 A-4C, BuNo 149644 WE/2, with black rudder and Blacksheep on the fuselage in 1968-69. (John Wible via Nick Williams) Below, VMA-214 A-4C, BuNo 150586 WE/1, at MCAS El Toro open house. (Mark Aldrich collection)

Capt Robert B. Beale was killed in BuNo 148585 when he was hit by small arms fire on a coastal reconnaissance mission near Tam Ky.

Upon returning to El Toro, the squadron's mission changed to that of the operational training squadron for attack pilots headed to Vietnam. During this period, Capt David W. Bittig was killed when his A-4C, BuNo 147769, crashed 218 miles north of Fallon during a navigation training flight on 15 July 1968. In November 1968, BuNo 148471 was stricken due to unknown causes. On 14 September 1969, MAJ Charles C. McLennan was killed in BuNo 149644 when he crashed during a cross country flight 15 miles northwest of Creede. Capt Robert P. Rogers was blown off the runway due to high winds at Yuma and crashed on landing in BuNo 148511 on 28 December 1969.

The A-4E replaced the C model in March 1970 and the A-4F was added in December 1970. In September 1972, the first Marine specific A-4M was acquired which was replaced with the AV-8B in June 1989.

MARINE ATTACK SQUADRON TWO-TWO-THREE, VMA-223 "BULLDOGS"

VMF-223 was formed on 1 May 1942 at NAS Barbers Point, TH, with Brewster F2A Buffalos. Flying the F4F-4 Wildcat, the "Rainbows" deployed aboard the USS Long Island and supported the August landings on Guadalcanal. The unit moved ashore on 20 August to Henderson Field. VMF-223 remained in combat until October, when they were withdrawn to San Diego for rest and retraining. The unit accounted for 83 enemy aircraft shot down, mostly by MAJ John Smith and Capt Marion Carl with just under twenty aircraft apiece.

The "Bulldogs", as they had become known, transitioned to the F4U-1 Corsair, in June, and moved to Efate, in the New Hebrides Island chain. They supported operations in Bougainville, Green Island, and Rabaul, before moving into the Philippines in January 1945. VMF-223 transitioned to the F4U-4 in May, and were supporting allied advances into Okinawa when the war ended. The Bulldogs accounted for 132.5 enemy aircraft shot down.

VMF-223 was moved to El Toro, CA, in March 1946, and then to MCAS Cherry Point, NC, in June 1948. They deployed to the Mediterranean in 1949, and returned in January of 1950. The unit entered the jet age in July, when they accepted the Grumman F9F-2 Panther.

The squadron deployed to NAS Atsugi, Japan, in September 1953, and were transferred to El Toro a year later. The Bulldogs were redesignated VMA-223 on 1 December 1954. The unit transitioned to the North American FJ-4B Fury in August 1957, and eventually switched to the A4D-

At top right, VMA-223 A4D-2N flightline at El Toro, CA, in 1961. (Paul Minert collection) Above right, VMA-223 A4D-2N, BuNo 147755 WP/5, on display on 19 August 1961. (Harry Gann) At right, the USS Yorktown with three VMA-223 Det T A-4Cs just forward of the island in 1964. Fin tip was red. (USN via Doug Siegfried)

2N (A-4C) in January 1961.

In April 1962, VMA-232 took its A-4Cs on two maneuvers. They participated in CASEX-1 (close air support exercise) at Twenty-Nine Palms and then an exercise in support of the 7th Marine Regiment at Camp Pendleton in late April. Also in 1962, they were the largest bond-selling squadron at El Toro with 55 of the unit's members buying bonds. In June, they had accumulated 12,000 accident-free flight hours, then on 5 November 1962, 1st LT Richard S. Horsfall was killed when he crashed in BuNo 148563.

Above, VMA-223 Det T A-4C, BuNo 148525 WP/82, on the port catapult aboard CVS-10 in 1964. Rudder trim and fuselage lightning bolt were green. (Doug Siegfried) Bottom, VMA-223 Det T A-4C, BuNo 147816 WP/85, taxis on the deck of CVS-10 in 1964 with Sidewinders. (Doug Siegfried)

On 4 February 1963, the squadron made a final weapons deployment to Yuma to prepare for its March deployment to Japan. At Yuma they practiced conventional and nuclear weapons delivery and helicopter escort techniques. In March 1963, their 13-month deployment to Iwakuni began. During this time, the squadron also operated from Okinawa and the Philippines. On 8 July 1963, 1st LT James E. Graham and MAJ William O. Bonsall were killed in a mid-air 17 miles north of Mt. Fuji while flying BuNos 147794 and 148451. In April 1964, the squadron began receiving A-4Es, however the unit continued to fly the A-4Cs, too, throughout 1964-65.

Above, four VMA-223 Det T A-4Cs, BuNos 148525 WP/82, 148501 WP/81, 150599 WP/84, and 148482 WP/83, on the deck of the USS Yorktown (CVS-10) in 1965. (USN via Doug Siegfried) Below, VMA-223 Det T A-4C, BuNo 147816 WP/85, awaits re-spotting on CVS-10 in 1965. (Doug Siegfried)

Four A-4Cs and six pilots were

aboard the USS Yorktown (CVS-10) from 23 October 1964 through 16 May 1965. During the cruise, CVS-10 spent 57 days on the line off Vietnam. On 7 December 1964, a Sidewinder missile mounted on BuNo 148482 ignited causing a jet fuel fire on the flight deck. Two VMA-223 men, CPL Reginald E. Matthews and PFC David F. Prince, were injured with 1st and 2nd degree burns and the aircraft was stricken. During the cruise, the six pilots made 1,200 carrier landings without a mishap.

In September 1965, the squadron deployed with its A-4Es to Iwakuni from where they rotated to Chu Lai on 15 December. The squadron departed Chu Lai and returned to Iwakuni on 4 December 1966, where they regrouped and flew A-4Cs. Then they returned to Chu Lai on 1 May 1967 with A-4Es once more. They returned to Iwakuni on 3 December 1967, where they re-equipped with A-4Cs before returning to Chu Lai on 23 April 1968 and in October inherited VMA-121 A-4Es .

On 6 May 1968, Capt Manual A. Guzman in A-4C, BuNo 145096 collided with MAJ Norman E. Pridgen from VMA-311 over the A Shau Valley. Both pilots ejected safely and were recovered by helicopter. Tragedy struck the squadron at Chu Lai when CPL Arthur L. Waldorf was critically burned in a flash fire at night during refueling. CPL Albert J. Faung was awarded the Navy and Marine

Above, VMA-223 Det T A-4C, BuNo 148482 WP/83, after a Sidewinder accidently ignited and burnt the outer left wing off on 7 December 1964 aboard CVS-10. (USN) Below, VMA-223 Det T A-4C, BuNo 148525 WP/82, traps on CVS-10 in 1965. (USN) Bottom, VMA-223 Det T A-4C, BuNo 150599 WP/84, took the barrier aboard (CVS-10) on 14 December 1964 after losing its tailhook on its previous landing attempt. (USN)

Above, VMA-223 A-4C, BuNo 147793 WP/6, at Udon in late 1968. Fin tip was yellow and black and aircraft has a VMA-311 wing tank. (Don Jay) Bottom, VMA-223 A-4C flightline at Chu Lai, Vietnam, on 4 May 1968. (USMC)

Corps Medal for his heroic attempt to save Waldorf from the flames. Then on 13 May 1968, Capt Steven J. Driscoll in BuNo 148549 was shot down near Tien Phuoc, 30 miles northwest of Chu Lai, where he ejected and was rescued safely by helicopter. On 6 June 1968, Capt Charles B. Coltrin's A-4C's left brake failed and the aircraft departed the runway and overturned. Coltrin was uninjured but the aircraft was stricken. 19 days later, Coltrin was hit by ground fire near Khe Sanh while flying BuNo 147804. He ejected safely and was rescued by helicopter. BuNo 147767 was lost on 1 October 1968 at Chu Lai when the left main tire blew on take-off and the aircraft crashed and burned. The pilot, 1st LT David I. Habemacher, was able to safely eject.

The squadron left Chu Lai for El Toro on 14 January 1970. On 31 July 1970, the squadron received the A-4F to complement its A-4Es. The unit moved to Yuma in June 1972 and received the A-4M in 1975.

MARINE ATTACK SQUADRON TWO-TWO-FOUR, VMA-224 "BENGALS"

On 1 May 1942, Marine Fighting Squadron 224 (VMF-224) was established at NAS Barbers Point, TH. Commanded by MAJ Robert E. Galer, Congressional Medal of Honor winner, and flying Grumman F4F Wildcats, VMF-224 was the second Marine fighter squadron to arrive on Guadalcanal during the Solomon Islands campaign. Re-equipped with Chance Vought F4U Corsairs, the unit took part in the battle for Okinawa. After a tour of occupation duty at Yokosuka, Japan, VMF-224 was assigned to MCAS Cherry Point, NC, and received F4U-5s. In 1949, McDonnell F2H-2 Banshees replaced the Corsairs and in 1952 these were replaced with Grumman F9F Panthers. The unit took its Panthers to Korea and was reassigned to MCAS El Toro, CA, in 1955 at the conclusion of its Far Eastern service. VMF-224 was redesignated VMA-224 and became the first Marine squadron to receive the Douglas A4D-1 Skyhawk in September 1956. In January 1959, the A4D-2 replaced the squadron's A4D-1s.

The A4D-2N (A-4C) replaced the squadron's A4D-2s in July 1961 while at MCAS Cherry Point, NC. In August, they began training for a deployment to Japan. In October through December 1961, the squadron deployed to NS Roosevelt Roads, PR, and Leaward Point, Cuba, for training and operations with the 14th Marine Expeditionary Unit. VMA-224 broke its own record by flying 1,427 flight hours in October and in November they participated in a naval show of force over the unstable capitol of the Dominican Republic. During December, carrier day and night qualifications were conducted aboard the USS Antietam and USS Franklin D. Roosevelt and the squadron completed over 13,000 accident free flight hours.

In 1962, while at Cherry Point, the squadron was awarded the fiscal 1962 Chief of Naval Operations Annual Aviation Safety Award and the Second Marine Aircraft Wing Commanding General's Outstanding Squadron Trophy was received on 19 July 1962.

Above, VMA-224 A4D-2N, BuNo 147779 WK/6, in the fall of 1962. Rudder segments were red. (K. Hyde via Norm Taylor) Below, VMA-224 A4D-2Ns, BuNos 148531 WK/12, 145143 WK/13, 147786 WK/14 and 148316 WK/21, in flight in late spring of 1962. Rudder trim was black. (Ginter collection)

In August 1962, VMA-224 deployed to MCAS Iwakuni, Japan. Soon after their arrival, the squadron departed for two weeks of maneuvers at Naha, Okinawa. Additional deployments were made to Cubi Point, Philippines, before returning to Cherry Point in October 1963. While in Japan, on 22 January 1963, 1st LT Jack R. Lousma ejected safely from his burning A-4C, BuNo 147716. Shortly after he ejected, the aircraft exploded in flight.

While back at Cherry Point, one A-4C was lost. On 25 October 1963, 1st LT Claiborne Brown ejected from BuNo 149548 and was killed when he ejected after an emergency belly landing in CASCO bay, ME. In June 1964, the squadron conducted carrier qualifications aboard the USS Saratoga (CVA-60). During these, on the 16th, VMA-224 set a all time high of 136 night traps in one night on a carrier. The squadron also received the Bullpup "Top Shot" award for USN and USMC squadrons.

During their March-April 1965 Yuma weapons deployment, six pilots received letters of commendation for professional excellence and outstanding airmanship. Then on 27 March 1965, 2nd LT Robert A. Kay, operating out of Yuma in BuNo 149487 crashed and was killed making a ground controlled approach to NAS Whidbey Island. He hit short of the runway and the aircraft flipped onto its back and caught fire.

On 2 October 1965, VMA-224 departed once again for Japan. Soon the squadron found itself at Chu Lai where they acquired ten A-4Es in December 1965. They continued to fly a small number of A-4Cs alongside of the A-4Es until 1 May 1966, when the unit was relocated to Iwakuni for two months while equipped with nineteen A-4Cs. When back at Chu Lai in July, they re-equipped with A-4Es again. On 1 November 1966, the squadron left Vietnam and returned to Cherry Point.

While back at Cherry Point, the squadron was redesignated VMA(AW)-224 and transitioned to the Grumman A-6 Intruder.

Above left, MAJ Levin in the cockpit of an A-4C at Chu Lai in 1965. (USMC) Below, VMA-224 flew a mixed bag of A-4C and A-4E aircraft in 1965-66. (USMC)

MARINE ATTACK SQUADRON TWO-TWO-FIVE, VMA-225 "VAGABONDS"

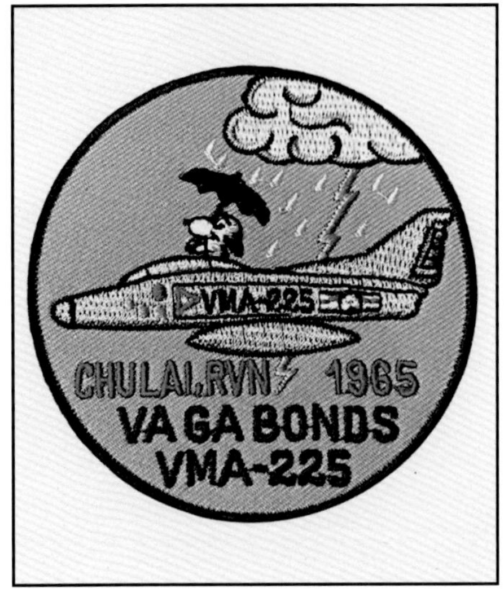

VMA-225 was established on 1 January 1943 and operated F4U Corsairs during WWII. The squadron was redesignated VMA-225 in June 1952 with AU-1 Corsairs. In 1954, Skyraiders replaced the AU-1s and in May 1958 the squadron transitioned to A4D-2 Skyhawks. On 11 March 1960, VMA-225 became the first Navy or Marine squadron to receive the new A4D-2N, BuNo 145086. Five more A4D-2Ns were received in March: BuNos 145076, 145089, 145097, 145098, and 145099. Eleven more were acquired in April and two in May.

The squadron's first A4D-2N, BuNo 145086, was lost on 21 July 1960 near Marquesas Key, west of Key West, FL. The pilot, 1st LT James C. Johnston, was killed when he crashed into the sea during a low-level stafing run.

The squadron joined CVG-10 aboard the USS Shangri-La (CVA-38) in September 1960 for a NATO cruise to England where they participated in NATO FALLEX 60 (Operation Swordthrust). It was a massive fleet exercise which included 60 ships and over 400 carrier-based aircraft. Aircraft carriers from the United States and the United Kingdom formed the major striking force, with escort cruisers, destroyers, submarines, and other escort ships. During the early stages of the operation, the Shangri-La launched nuclear attacks against the continent from the Norwegian Sea and later launched simulated conventional attacks deep into Europe in support of ground operations. After the exercise, CVG-10 returned to Mayport where it answered an alert called by President Eisenhower to stage a show-of-force to curb communist aggression. The ship and CVG-10 were given 12-hours notice and conducted operations off the coast of Guatemala and Nicaragua.

In February 1961, CVA-38 and VMA-225 sailed for a Mediterranean cruise which lasted until August 1961. Ports-of-call were: Rota, Naples, Rome, Pompeii, Cannes, Paris, Istanbul, Rhodes, Malta, Barcelona, and Gibraltar. During the cruise, Capt

Below, VMA-225 A4D-2N, BuNo 145104 CE/13, armed with rocket pods in 1960. (USMC)

Above, VMA-225 A4D-2N, BuNo 145105 CE/11, in flight in 1960 while armed with rocket pods. Rudder segments were black. (Ginter collection) Below, VMA-225 A4D-2N, BuNo 147724 AK/600, catapults off CVA-38 in March 1961. (USN via Mark Aldrich) Bottom, VMA-225 A4D-2N, BuNo 145114 AK/604, in flight while assigned to the USS Shangri-La (CVA-38) in 1961-62. (USN via Peter Mersky collection)

Walter W. Hargidine was lost overboard in BuNo 145098 on 15 February 1961 upon lauching while in the Med. On 6 April 1961, BuNo 145107 AK/610, was lost after landing on CVA-38. Capt McCarthy was taxiing forward when his throttle stuck and he motored over the side. The A-4C landed right side up in the water and McCarthy ejected the canopy and tried to climb out. His oxygen hose stopped him and he had get down into the cockpit to disconnect it. He was retrieved safely and resumed to flight ops the next day.

On 31 October 1961, after returning to CONUS, BuNo 145089 was stricken for unknown reasons. Then, from 26 December 1961 through 2 March 1962, the squadron deployed

to Roosevelt Roads for weapons training on the ranges at Vieques Island. While there, Capt Willard Wyatt in BuNo 145134 and 1st LT Richard J. Morgart in 147676 were missing after being involved in a mid-air ten miles south of Guantanamo Bay. On 27 February 1962, another A4D-2 (A-4C) was stricken for unknown reasons.

In October through December 1962, VMA-225 was drafted aboard the USS Enterprise (CVAN-65) as an additional attack squadron to CVW-6's VA-66 and VA-76 during the Cuban Missile Crisis. From 29 January to 27 February 1963, the squadron made another weapons deployment to Rosey Roads, PR. After returning to Cherry Point, 1st LT James R. Foster was killed when he ejected from BuNo 148315 and his chute failed to open. He ejected over a woody swamp near Scotland Neck, NC, in his smoking Skyhawk after flying away from an inhabited area. Another pilot and aircraft were lost on 3 March 1964 when Capt Jack C. Kennedy ejected from BuNo 147800 on landing at Cherry Point.

In September 1964, VMA-225 deployed to MCAS Iwakuni, Japan. While there they also conducted operations from Cubi Point, Naha, Kadina, Seoul, and Bankok. 1st LT John H. Floyd was killed on 8 February 1965 in BuNo 148522 while on a practice bombing mission off the coast of Korea. Then, in May 1965, VMA-225 was ordered to Vietnam.

Above left, VMA-225 A4D-2N, BuNo 145107 AK/610, taxied off CVA-38's deck when its throttle stuck on 11 April 1961. (USN) Above right, the pilot, Capt McCarthy, was rescued by the plane-guard helicopter and is seen being helped across the deck. (USN) Below, VMA-225 A-4C, BuNo 145106 CE/20, in 1962 with squadron insignia on the vertical tail and a barber-striped refueling probe. (Ginter collection) Bottom, VMA-225 A-4C, BuNo 148531 CE/12, in May 1964. (Nick Williams collection)

The first operational A-4Cs to operate from Chu Lai SATS field landed on 1 June 1965, less than a month after construction of the airfield began. The first flight to land were four aircraft from VMA-225. The pilots in order of landing were: COL John D. Noble, CO of MAG-12; LCOL Robert W. Baker, CO of VMA-225; MAJ Donald E. Gillum; and MAJ David A. Teichmann. At 13:15 hours, the four aircraft lead by Baker conducted air

Above, VMA-225 A-4Cs, BuNos 147776 CE/2, 147709 CE/13, 145131 CE/16, and 145121 CE/19, in flight on 31 August 1964. (USMC) Bottom, VMA-225 A-4C, BuNo 147767 CE/3, making a JATO take-off with a light load of bombs from Chu Lai. (Peter Mersky collection)

strikes six miles from the field in support of ARVAN units. JATO was used to launch the Skyhawks until May 1966 when a SATS catapult was installed.

The Marines' first big offensive was Operation Starlight on 18 and 19 August 1965, which was heavily supported by Marine air assets. Three A-4C squadrons were involved: VMA-214, VMA-225, and VMA-311. These three Skyhawk squadrons along with two F-4B squadrons, VMFA-342 and VMFA-513, flew 78 sorties the first day. Ordnance expended included 65 tons of bombs, 4 tons of napalm, 523 2.75-inch rockets, and 6,000 rounds of 20mm. Although successful, the operation was extended and in three days, the fixed wing assets flew more sorties than any other attack groups in Marine history. During Starlight operations less than a dozen miles south of Chu Lai, the Marine aircraft operated on a constant flight pattern of take-off, drop ordanance, fire rockets and straf, land, rearm, and do it again.

VMA-225 became VMA(AW)-225 on 5 April 1966 and was disestablished on 15 June 1975.

Above, Chu Lai with VMA-225 A-4Cs on the ramp. (Mark Aldrich collection) Bottom, VMA-225 A-4C, BuNo 148520 CE/13, in the SATS gear at Chu Lai. VMA-225 was the first squadron to operate from Chu Lai. (Ginter collection)

MARINE ATTACK SQUADRON TWO-FOUR-TWO, VMA-242

VMA-242 originally was established as Marine Torpedo Bombing Squadron Two Hundred Forty-Two (VMTB-242) on 1 July 1943 at El Centro, CA. Flying the TBM/TBF Avenger aircraft, the squadron deployed to Espiritu Santo, New Herbrides, in the Southwest Pacific aboard the USS Kitum Bay (CVE-71) in February 1944. They operated in the Northern Solomons, Saipan, Tinian and Iwo Jima. In November 1945, they returned to San Diego and were deactivated on 23 November.

On 1 October 1960, the unit was reactivated as Marine Attack Squadron Two Hundred Forty-Two (VMA-242) at MCAS Cherry Point, NC, with the A4D-2 Skyhawk. As sometimes happens, their first aircraft was received before the official establishment date. The first A4D-2 arrived on 12 June 1960, followed by one in August and then twelve more after establishment. In December 1960, the unit received eleven A4D-2Ns and flew both the A4D-2 and the A4D-2N through September 1961 when the last nine A4D-2s were transferred out.

While at Cherry Point, on 29 November 1961, 1st LT Daniel J. Hampton safely ejected from A4D-2N, BuNo 147831, after a flameout and several attempts at a re-start. That same day, 1st LT Charles A. Brunt in BuNo 145138 and Capt Harris J. Fennell in 147684 collided over the Newport River. Brunt was killed after ejecting and Fennell was able to safely eject. Two days later, on 1 December 1961, 1st LT C.H. Brown was killed in the crash of BuNo 147770 near Russell, AR. He was part of a three-plane cross-country flight from Cherry Point to Buckley Field, Denver, CO. The reason for the crash was not known. Due to the Cuban Missile Crisis, VMA-242 deployed to NAS Key West, FL, in October 1962. They returned to Cherry Point in late November 1962, where they lost two more A-4Cs and one pilot. 1st LT Floyd K. Wright was killed in BuNo 148604 during a night rocket and bombing training mission northeast of Morehead City on 16 January 1963. Then on 7 February 1963, 2nd LT Charles R. Connor ejected safely from BuNo 145146 after colliding with Capt Frederick R. Jerrett in 148505. The planes collided over Cherry Point and Jerrett was able to land safely.

VMA-242 deployed to NAS Iwakuni, Japan, in October 1963. During their year in Japan, they also operated from Cubi Point and Okinawa. The squadron returned to Cherry Point in September 1964 where they were redesignated VMA(AW)-242 and transitioned to the new A-6A Intruder. In December

Below, VMA-242 A-4C, BuNo 147777 DT/12, armed with Bullpups and napalm in 1960. Rudder segments were red as were barber pole stripes on the refueling probe. (Harry Gann)

Above, VMA-242 A4D-2N flightline in 1961 with BuNo 147672 DT/5, in the foreground. (USMC) At right, four VMA-242 A4D-2Ns, BuNos 148511 DT/3, 148514 DT/9, 148533 DT/2, and 145145 DT/5 in flight. (USMC) Bottom, VMA-242 A-4C, BuNo 145103 DT/5, dropping a napalm bomb during weapons training in Okinawa on 7 July 1964. (USN)

1990, they were redesignated VMFA(AW)-242 and were equipped with F/A-18D Hornets.

MARINE ATTACK SQUADRON THREE-ONE-ONE, VMA-311 "TOMCATS"

VMF-311 was formed on 1 December 1942 at MCAS Cherry Point, NC, and initially equipped with North American SNJ trainers. The unit received the Vought F4U-1 Corsair in April 1943 and moved to Page Field on Parris Island, SC. The squadron went to the South Pacific in August, and eventually arrived on Wallis Island, before moving to Samoa in January 1944. VMF-311 participated in the Marshall Islands campaign during 1944, and the Okinawa campaign in 1945. The squadron accounted for 71 enemy aircraft shot down.

After the war ended, the unit was moved to the West Coast, before settling at El Toro, CA, in September 1946. VMF-311 became the West Coast's first jet squadron, on 20 July 1948, when they accepted a pair of Lockheed TO-1 Shooting Stars. The unit adopted the nickname, "Willy Lovers" to represent the phonetic pronunciation of their "WL" tail code. The Grumman F9F-2B Panther replaced the TO-1 in March 1950.

The unit arrived in Yokosuka, Japan, in November 1950 and departed for Korea in December. The squadron flew close air support combat missions with the F9F-5 during the Korean War and returned to El Toro in May 1955. The Tomcats upgraded to the F9F-8 Cougar in March 1957, and were redesignated VMA-311 on 1 June 1957.

The Tomcats began their affiliation with the Douglas Skyhawk in 1958, when they accepted the A4D-2. VMA-311 moved to MCAS Yuma, AZ, in 1959, and TransPac'd to NAS Atsugi, Japan, in March 1961. The Tomcats returned to El Toro in March 1962 and upgraded to the A-4E in June 1963. They flew their 15,000th accident-free hour in October.

The unit TransPac'd to Iwakuni on 1 April 1964 with twenty A-4Es. VMA-311 then deployed eight of the A-4Es to Chu Li, Vietnam, on 24 May 1965. The first four aircraft arrived on 1 June 1965. These eight aircraft were supplemented by four A-4Cs, BuNos 147782, 148465, 148518 and 148595, assigned to the squadron at Chu Lai. 148595 was destroyed on the ground during a Viet Cong raid on the base on 28 October 1965.

On 15 December 1965, VMA-311 rotated back to Iwakuni with VMA-223 taking their place. At Iwakuni, the squadron was assigned eleven A-4Cs for training purposes. Then, after incorporating and training some replacement pilots, the squadron returned to Chu Lai on 15 February 1966.

Upon arrival at Chu Lai, they were assigned eleven different A-4Cs to operate alongside the squadron's A-4Es. However, the A-4Cs only operated through June 1966 before being completely replaced with the Echos.

Two A-4C aircraft were lost on this second round of operations from Chu Li. On 9 March 1966, 1st LT Augusto M. "Gussie" Xavier was

Below, the 4th A4D-2N built, BuNo 145065 WL/4, was briefly assigned to VMA-311. Fin tip and rudder were red. (Harry Gann)

Above, VMA-311 A-4C, BuNo 148472 WL/1, seen at Yokota AB, Japan, on 20 May 1967, was the CO's aircraft. The rudder segments were red and orange-yellow and "Topcat" on the nose was red. (Toyokazu Matsuzaki) Below, two VMA-311 A-4Cs (ex VMA-225) sit in their makeshift revetments at Chu Lai in September 1965. (USMC)

killed when he flew BuNo 148518 into the side of a mountain while providing support for a Green Beret unit and ARVN troops in the A-Shau Valley in a pre-dawn strike. A-4C, BuNo 147808, was being returned by helicopter to Chu Lai on 5 May 1966 for repairs when it became unstable and was destroyed when it was jettisoned.

VMA-311 was relieved in March 1967. When they arrived at Iwakuni, they received twenty-five A-4Cs for use in training while in Japan, Okinawa and Cubi Point. The squadron then returned to Chu Lai in June 1967 where they flew the A-4E.

The squadron continued to fly the A-4E until 1 September 1974 when they transitioned to the A-4M Skyhawk at MCAS Beaufort, SC. The AV-8B Harrier replaced the A-4Ms in June1988.

MARINE ATTACK SQUADRON THREE-TWO-TWO, VMA-322 "FIGHTING GAMECOCKS"

VMF-322 was established at MCAS Cherry Point, NC, on 1 July 1943, and subsequently moved to Parris Island, SC. They left Page Field in January 1944 and eventually arrived at Emirau in September. Flying the F4U-1/1D and FG-1D Corsair, the "Fighting Cocks" supported operations from Okinawa in 1945. The unit moved to Midway Island in November with brand new Vought F4U-4 Corsairs. In July 1947, the "Fighting Cocks" transferred to MCAS Ewa, TH, in July 1947. In April 1949, the squadron returned to the US and was disestablished at MCAS Edenton, NC, on 30 November 1949.

VMF-322 was reactivated on 6 July 1951 as a Marine Reserve unit at NARF Squantum, MA, and moved to NAS South Weymouth, MA, in 1953. The Grumman F9F-6 Cougar replaced the F4U-4 in January 1954. The unit was redesignated VMA-322 in May 1958, and changed their name to "Fighting Gamecocks". The North American FJ-3 replaced the Cougar in November 1959.

The Squadron accepted the Douglas A-4C Skyhawk in September 1962. The A-4Cs were replaced with A-4Es in 1973 which in turn were replaced with A-4Ms in May 1983. The squadron also acquired a few TA-4Js in 1980 and a few TA-4Fs in 1989. The unit was disestablished on 27 June 1992.

While flying the A-4Cs, two aircraft were lost. The first, BuNo 147775, was stricken after a ground accident on 18 August 1971. The second was lost on 7 December 1975 during an ACM training flight. Capt Andrew J. Ley ejected safely from BuNo 150135 which had entered an unrecoverable spin and crashed in a wooded area near Colebrook, NH.

Above, VMA-322 A-4C, BuNo 148571 5Z/57, at NAS Quonset Point, RI, on 5 June 1971. Rudder trim was black. (Tom Cuddy) Below, VMA-322 A-4C, BuNo 148571 QR/57, taxiing at NAS South Weymouth in 1972. (Tom Hildreth) Bottom, VMA-322 A-4C, BuNo 145068 QR/58, at McChord AFB, WA, on 9 December 1972. (Doug Remington via Norm Taylor)

MARINE ATTACK SQUADRON THREE-TWO-FOUR, VMA-324 "DEVILDOGS"

Above, VMA-324 A-4C, BuNo 150583 DX/21, on display at Robins AFB, GA, in May 1969. (Wally Gilbaugh via Norm Taylor) Below, VMA-324 A-4C, BuNo 148501 DX/8, conducts a JATO take-off in late 1968. (USMC)

VMF-324 originally was formed on 1 October 1943 at MCAS Cherry Point, NC, and was equipped with the Vought F4U-1 and Goodyear FG-1. The unit eventually was moved to Midway in September 1944 and was brought back to MCAS Miramar, CA, a year later and deactivated on 15 October 1945.

VMF-324 was reactivated on 17 March 1952 at NAS Cherry Point, NC, and flew a mixed-bag of Goodyear FG-1s and Grumman F6F Hellcats. The unit was moved to MCAS Miami, FL, in April. In November, the unit was redesignated VMA-324 and assigned Vought AU-1 Corsairs and Douglas AD-4B Skyraiders. In October 1953, the "Vagabonds" loaded their assortment of AD-4/4B/4L Skyraiders aboard the USS Saipan (CVS-48) for a WestPac cruise, returning to Miami in July 1954. VMA-324 deployed to the Med aboard the USS Lake Champlain (CVA-39) from September 1955 to April 1956. Upon their return, the unit transitioned to the AD-6 Skyraider before transitioning to the Douglas A4D-2 Skyhawk in May 1959.

They took their Skyhawks aboard the USS Coral Sea (CVA-43) from September 1960 to May 1961 before making another deployment aboard the USS Independence (CVA-62) from August 1963 to March 1964. Upon return to the US, the squadron transitioned to the A-4E. With the A-4E, the squadron deployed aboard "Indy" from 13 June 1966 to 1 February 1967.

In July 1968, the squadron traded in their A-4Es for sixteen A-4Cs. In June 1970, the A-4E replaced the A-4Cs and the A-4M was acquired in April 1971. On 29 August 1974 VMA-324 was deactivated.

While flying the A-4C, on 6 June

1970, 1st LT Thomas Boyd ejected safely when the brakes failed on BuNo 149535 while landing at the El Paso International Airport. The aircraft crashed through the fence and onto Airport Road.

Above, VMA-324 A-4C, BuNo 145064 DX/1, with red rudder and white trim in June 1969. It was the 3rd A-4C built. (Harry Gann) Below, VMA-324 flightline with A-4C, BuNo 147722 DX/5, in the foreground. (Peter Mersky collection) Bottom, VMA-324 A-4C, BuNo 148575 DX/11, on 20 May 1969. (Harry Gann)

MARINE ATTACK SQUADRON THREE-THREE-TWO, VMA-332 "POLKADOTS"

Below, VMA-332 A-4C, BuNo 145145 EA/12, in 1962-63. Rudder trim and drop tank trim were red. (Paul McDaniel vim Jim Sullivan) Bottom, VMA-332 pilots pose in front of A-4C, BuNo 148508 EA/10, in August 1962. Kneeling L-to-R: Prigmore, Scarborough, Morgan, LCOL McDaniel (CO), MAJ Peacock (XO), Schwab, and Padios. Standing L-to-R: Edens, Barbosa, Dixen, Floyd, Walker, Wright, James, Emery, Cark, Clapp, and Morrison. (USMC via Tailhook)

VMSB-332 was activated at MCAS Cherry Point, NC, on 1 June 1943 and assigned Douglas SBD Dauntless dive bombers. The unit moved to MCAS Mojave in January 1944 before moving to MCAS Ewa, TH, in February 1945. The following month, they transferred to Midway Island before returning to Ewa in July to transition to the Curtiss SB2C dive bomber. The squadron was redesignated VMTB-332 in March 1945 and operated the TBM Avenger until the unit was deactivated on 13 November 1945.

After a combat tour in Korea, the Polka Dots returned to Miami, FL, in December of 1953 and transitioned to the AD-4 Skyraider. The unit later upgraded to the AD-5 and AD-6 before accepting the Douglas A4D-2 in 1958.

They upgraded to the A4D-2N (A-4C) on 13 October 1960 when fourteen were acquired. Four more were added in November and ten in December. The squadron rotated to Japan in 1961 and was ordered to Udorn, Thailand, as a show-of-force from April through August 1962. They were part of JTF-116 which included 3,000 men of the 3rd Marine Expeditionary Bridgade. Luckily, no combat action occurred.

Four incidents occurred during the squadron's first assignment of A4D-2Ns/A-4Cs from 1960 through 1964. The 1st was a ground handling accident on 5 November 1960 when BuNo 147757 was stricken. Then the MAG-12 XO, LCOL Arthur W. Nehf, ejected safely from BuNo 148539 near Iwakuni, Japan; on 5 December 1961 when he experienced a low-altitude flame-out. On 23 April 1962, 1st LT Norman F. Suedekum was killed in BuNo 147778 during SEATO Exercise Air Cobra. 1st LT Frederick R. Harshbarger in BuNo 145130 was involved in a mid-air with 2nd LT James Barbosa in 147774 on 11 April 1964. The accident near Cherry Point left Harshbarger with a back injury while Barbosa was unhurt.

Five A-4Es were received on 22 July 1964, followed by one in August, four in October, nine in November, and two in December. In October 1966, most of the A-4Es were replaced with fifteen A-4Cs. By January 1967 all the A-4Es were gone. Then on 20 August 1968, in preparation for receiving A-6 Intruders, VMA-332 was redesignated VMA(AW)-332. The A-4Cs gradually were replaced with Grumman A-6Es, with the last A-4C being trans-

Above, VMA-332 A-4C, BuNo 150599 EA/00, in 1966-68 with red rudder trim. (via Harry Gann) At right, VMA-332 A-4C Snoopy nose art seen on 30 May 1967. (William Swisher) Bottom, VMA-332 A-4C, BuNo 149541 EA/7, at Cherry Point in 1966-68. (Harry Gann)

ferred out in September 1968.

Three A-4Cs were lost during this period, the first on 8 February 1967. 2nd LT K.W. Kwmch ejected safely 10 miles south of Cherry Point from BuNo 149582 after receiving a fire warning light. Then, on 17 August 1967, Capt Michael Sandlin in BuNo 148506 and Capt Paul Witting in 149610 collided northeast of Cherry Point. Both pilots ejected safely, but the incident ended Witting's career.

MARINE ATTACK SQUADRON FIVE-THREE-THREE, VMA-533 "NIGHTHAWKS"

VMA-533 originally was established as VMF(N)-533 on 1 October 1943 with F6F-5N night fighters. They were the Marine's third such squadron of night fighters to be organized in WWII. In April 1944, the squadron reached the West Coast and embarked on the USS Long Island (CVE-1). On 6 May, the unit arrived at Eniwetok where they relieved VMF(N)-532 and assumed the night defense of the area. In November, the squadron moved to Engebi where they stayed until June of 1945 when they trasferred to Le Shima. On 14 July, the outfit moved to Chimu on Okinawa where they remained until the wars end. When the war ended, VMA-533 had 35 kills to its credit, more than any other US night fighter squadron.

From October 1945 through January 1947, the squadron remained at Chimu. The squadron transferred in February 1947 to Cherry Point, NC, where they acquired the Grumman F7F Tigercat. During the Korean War the squadron remained at Cherry Point where they trained all-weather fighter pilots. These pilots were sent to Korea individually upon completion of their training.

After the Korean War, the Tigercats were replaced with the McDonnell F2H Banshee before receiving F9F Cougars in September 1956. The Cougars were replaced with A4D-2 Skyhawks in August 1959 and VMF-533 was redesignated VMA-533. Fifteen A4D-2Ns arrived in late September and early October 1960 to replace the A4D-2s. They were only on hand for about 30-days before being pulled and replaced with A4D-2s again. In February 1964, twenty-five A-4Cs once again replaced the A-4Bs at VMA-533. A little over a year later, on 1 July 1965, they were redesignated VMA(AW)-533 and transitioned to the A-6A Intruder.

During the squadron's 1960 stint with the A4D-2N, BuNo 147705 was lost on 20 September with just 39-hours of flight time on the airframe. Four VMA-533 pilots were practicing high dive bomb delivery maneuvers for nuclear weapons over the Pamlico Sound bombing range using six Mk-76 practice bombs. 2nd LT Robert H. Melville had made five runs and began his sixth and final run at 24,000 feet by applying right aileron to roll the aircraft inverted. It immediately went into a sustained right roll and dive. All efforts by the pilot to overcome this roll proved futile and he ejected at 15,000 feet. The ejection proved to be the first successful RAPEC (rocket assisted personnel ejection catapult) rocket egress system ejection. On 1 November 1964, Capt W.A. Cason ejected from BuNo 149637 300 miles east of the Azores while flying from Cherry Point to Spain. He was rescued by the SS Zoella Lykes.

Below, VMA-533 A4D-2N, BuNo 145081 ED/1, in 1964 after being zapped with measles by VMGR-252. (via Tailhook)

MARINE ATTACK SQUADRON FIVE-FOUR-THREE, VMA-543

Marine Night Fighter Squadron Five Hundred Forty-Three (VMF(N)-543) was established on 15 April 1944 at MCAS Cherry Point, NC. The "NightHawks" were assigned Grumman F6F-3N and F6F-5N Hellcats before transferring to MCAS El Centro, CA. The squadron was split into three sections and sent separately to Awase Airfield on Okinawa where they were deactivated after the war.

VMF-543 was reactivated in the '50s as a reserve unit at NAS Glenview, IL, where they flew F8F-1s and F9F-6s until becoming VMA-543. They received A-4Bs in the early 1960s which were replaced with A-4Ls in 1970-71. The squadron was de-activated in 1974.

Above, VMA-543 A-4L, BuNo 145114 MD/11, in 1972. (Fred Roos) Below, VMA-543 A-4L, BuNo 145119 MD/3, in 1972. 5119 on the dorsal fin was in red. (Fred Roos) Bottom, VMA-543 A-4L, BuNo 145122 MD/4, at NAS Alameda, CA, on 7 September 1973. Wing tips were yellow and rudder segments were yellow and black. (Gary Verver collection)

PACIFIC MISSILE CENTER, NAS POINT MUGU

Established in 1946, the Naval Air Missile Test Center became the Naval Missile Center (NMC) in 1959 and the Pacific Missile Test Center (PMTC) in 1975. The basic mission of the Naval Missile Center was to integrate new and existing missile systems into the fleet. Not all aircraft came from Navy stocks, some came from the Marines too.

Below, A-4C, BuNo 145071 (at right), while assigned to the Pacific Missile Center (PMC) on 11 December 1964 with A-4B, BuNo 142709 (at left). The vertical tail, nose and outer wing panels were da-glo red. (USN) Bottom, the Flying Brothers Team, three Navy and three Marine pilots, pose in front of one of their VMA-224 A-4Cs, BuNo 145065, in 1963. The "7" on the fuselage side was red, all other markings were black. (via Tailhook)

7th FLEET FLYING BROTHERS

In the early 1960s, the 7th Fleet's Flying Brothers flew VMA-224 A-4Cs in the annual US/Asian Fighter Weapons Conference held at Clark AFB, PI. Teams were from the USAF, USN/USMC, Thailand, Australia, Nationalist China and the Philippines. The team of six were made up of 1/2 USN and 1/2 USMC pilots and defeated the other team's F-84s, F-86s, and F-100s.

MARINE A-4C/L DISPLAY AIRCRAFT